Edition : Books on Demand,
12/14 rond-Point des Champs-Elysées, 75008 Paris
Impression : BoD - Books on Demand, Norderstedt, Allemagne
ISBN : 9782322220465
Dépôt légal : Mai 2020

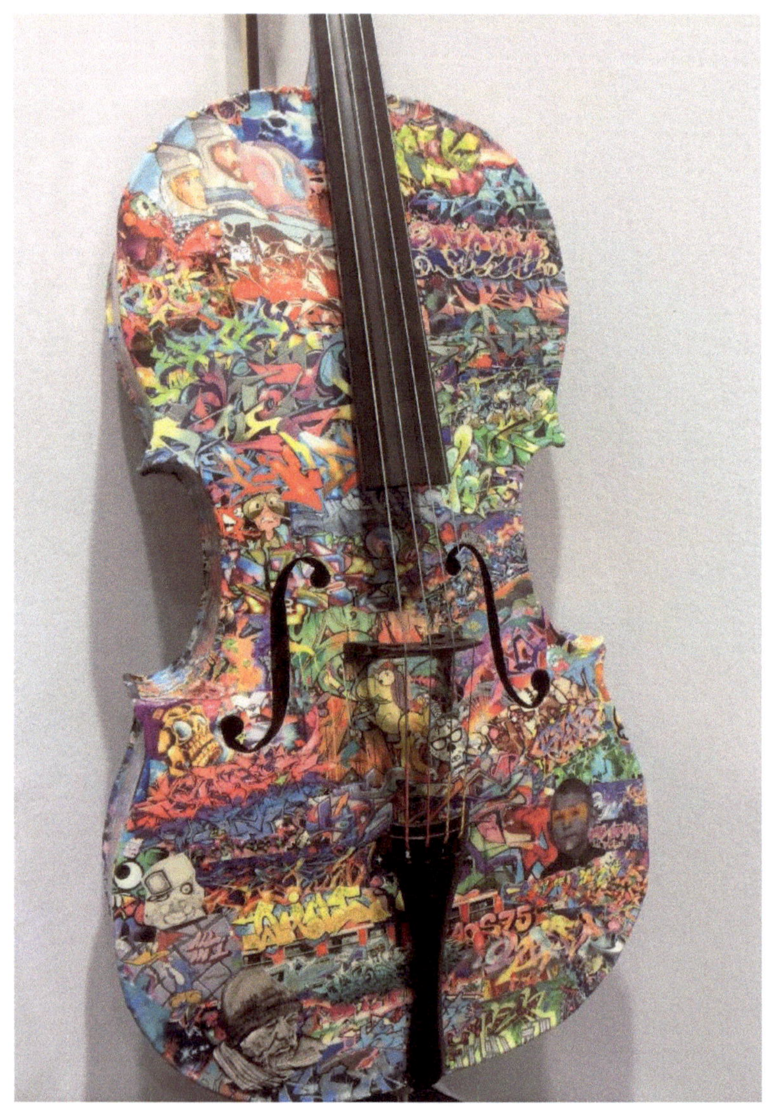

TABLE OF CONTENTS

1 Academism or not?

- The advantages of the cello compared to other stringed instruments

2 Recommendations and prerequisites

- Who is this guide for?
- The choice of the instrument
- The instrument maker - his role
- The budget
- Time available - when to play?
- The room where to play music. How should it be ?

3 The basics of your learning

- A bit of music theory - choice of scales to start
- A bit of music theory - the left hand and the finger position
- A bit of music theory - the movement of the bow and the rhythm.
- To define the content of the lessons when starting

4 The practice

- The position

- To know how to install the strings and how to tune the cello

- Downloadable scores and accompanying music

- How to Carry your instrument -transport in a plane

- How to organize your musical session

- How to decrypt a new score - improvement of your practice

- Playing with other musicians in a group

- Technological means available in website for practice improvement

Fingering of other scales suggested

Anatomy of the instrument

Proposals of music scores and methods

- Scores that can be downloaded

- Scores dedicated for beginners

1 Academism or not?

You decided to play the cello because you were seduced last summer by a string quartet concert, which you attended in an enchanting setting. Or you inherited a string instrument which was forgotten in an attic for fifty years. You are retired and you want to start learning a music instrument ... but so far you have never dared to do it

Academism or not? For an adult, the question really arises and the music academic school or the music conservatory is far from the only solution for learning and maintaining the pleasure of playing. Ask the question in your surroundings. Who attended the music conservatory and who still regularly practices the instrument? You will find that the vast majority gave up on the pretext of lack of time. But in reality, it is probably the lack of enthusiasm due to this academic learning or simply the logic of selection of the best musicians who is the cause. Could not the conservatory's motto be summed up as "excellence or nothing"?

But except for registration in a city public music conservatory or a private conservatory, you do not see how to concretely proceed. Very quickly, you were asked about your knowledge of music theory and you feel that you do not have the required level. Is there available room in adult classes? The schedule and the day of availability of the lessons on Friday from 20:00 to 22:00 do not suit you ... Finally the cost of the instrument and the registration to the course make you think. Can a cello be transported otherwise than in a heavy and voluminous "knight armor" ?

All these obstacles naturally stop you to take the plunge.

This approach is there to encourage you to try if you accept to "ignore" the works of the 19th and 20th century in your potential repertoire. I mean the works you would not be able to play because they require a real knowledge of music theory. For the baroque repertoire that is within your school solfege level, it will take a little daring and perseverance. What are the real prerequisites?

* **A room** where you plan to play regularly. It must be sufficiently insulated phonetically (neighbors) if you live in a condo, and big enough to get the fullness of sound. Mute abstain! It inhibits the musician and also the instrument,

* **An instrument maker** whom you have already pushed the door and whom you trust. A good instrument maker is almost more useful than a good teacher because teachers, you will change. The instrument maker knows your instrument and will know how to compensate for any sound defects.

* **A basic level of music theory**. The level acquired at the college is enough to play composed pieces until the end of the eighteenth century or current variety themes.

* **A three-month availability of time** to start and take your first lessons. This is necessary to acquire with your teacher, but mostly by yourself, a minimum of accuracy and fingering of the 3 most common scales. 5 to 10 lessons might be sufficient for starting your self-learning…but with assistance anyway.

* **A music instrument**. This one can be rented if you are not sure of your future involvement any longer in cello practice. If you decide to buy, start with a "study" cello.

After that, you can go to the Kerguelen Islands or Patagonia and do your practice by yourself …

Later, you will challenge yourself because you will really be bitten. It is the desire to play more difficult but beautiful works that will make you take other lessons to progress.

The advantages of the cello compared to other stringed instruments

Two factors contribute to the choice of the cello:

• The tone of the instrument: An instrument for treble sound (the violin is dedicated to the SOL clef) is not very acceptable for listening in case of a mistake of accuracy. If you do not perform the finger position of the left hand properly, it will result in an unpleasant sound, which besides your neighbors will tire you. The practice of the violin may discourage you even before you have acquired the correctness of performance. To be convinced of this, it is enough to observe the number of old violins to sell in the markets or antique shops . The cello of medium tone (it is centered on the clef of FA) is more rewarding and encouraging to the game. It will tolerate more easily an approximate fingering, except in high pitched sounds obviously. However, you will find it harder to find a cello teacher than a violin teacher.

• The ergonomic related to the holding of the instrument: The way to hold the instrument is not immutable and has evolved over the centuries. The cello was held vertically and resting on a cushion in Lully's time. Subsequently, his outfit was closer to that of the "viola da gamba", so between the legs. An endpin was added so that it could be held at the desired height and inclination.

The violin stands today in two different ways. The European outfit which requires for playing to rotate the wrist. In this position; I invite you to try to handle a violin to realize, it is relatively difficult to press forcefully with the 4th finger and all the more so, if you have to do it on the fourth string. By simulating this position, one easily realizes the ergonomic difficulty that it presents. Do not we often hear novice violinists say that they have to work the dexterity of the 4th finger?

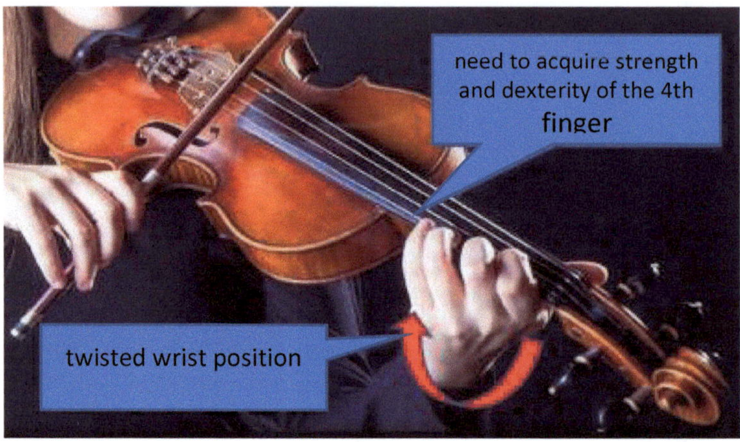

Some Hindus who practice the violin have adopted a different, more ergonomic position. They play squatting and hold the violin vertically by placing it on the calf. The problem of twisting of the wrist is thus avoided. The Chinese also have a string instrument called "ehru", a distant cousin of the violin, which they hold in the same way.

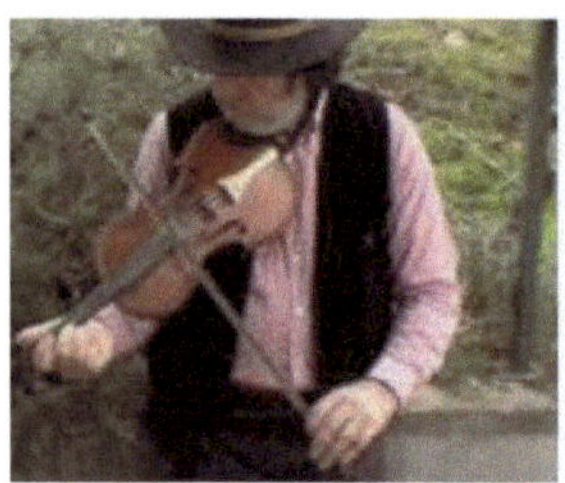 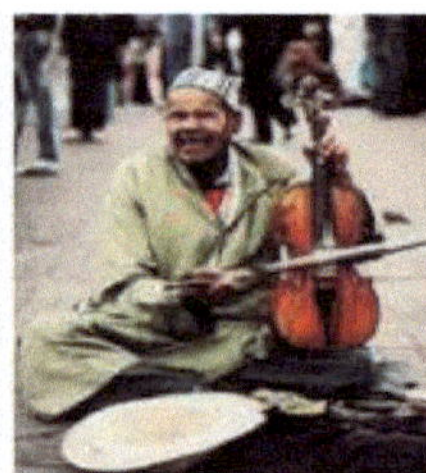 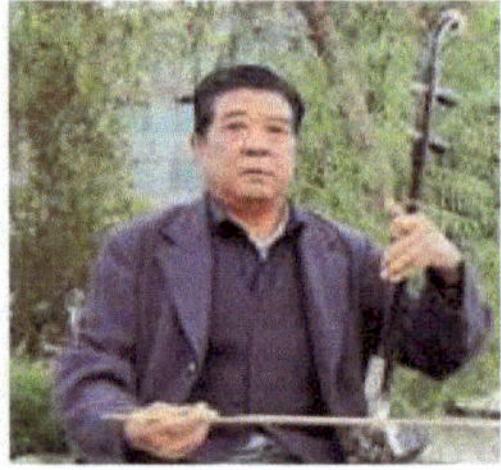

Gypsies practice the violin with an incomparable dexterity (let us remember Ivry Gitlis). They play by rotating the violin soundboard inward along its longitudinal axis. Thus, the twist of the wrist is reduced

2 Recommendations and prerequisites.

Who is this guide for?

To adults, music lovers who aspire above all to give themselves the pleasure of discovering and playing an instrument. You are not in the norm and conventions. So this guide is dedicatedly yours. I assure you, no need for years of music theory is required. You do not need the fastidious manner of course taught by the music conservatory teachers. You don't want to hear any longer remarks as "you did not work the beat and the bow movement since the last session" ... when you spent already three hours there. How many young apprentice musicians gave up while they already acquired a practice quite sufficient to be able to play, a repertoire very consequent ?

Why learning to play hard pieces as the concerto of Chostakovich or the one of Ravel, or the prelude of the fourth Suite of Bach ? If you are satisfied with older pieces, there is a whole baroque repertoire, including the first three Bach Suites, which you could play and which do not require, whatever you think about it, particular virtuosity in playing.

The cello is for me close of wind instruments in the sense that we can produce with it only successive notes and not simultaneous ones, unlike the piano or even the guitar. To affirm this, just notice that the music scores for bassoon and for cello are identical. Of course, there are in cello pieces double strings and trills. But this is not the majority of the game.

Another analogy is that the sound of the cello needs to be "fabricated" by your own. With the right hand, the movement of the bow, can be fast or slow, pulled or pushed, soft or with an attack, strong or light, with linked or separated notes for the game of a triplet.

With the left hand, with or without vibrato, according to the choice of the position. So there is an infinite possibility of producing notes. Moreover, a rich repertoire accessible for a beginner does not require virtuosity of the game. I mean by this that the speed in the execution is far from being the rule. We can therefore devote all the pleasure and time for producing a rich sound. The instrument, as long as you play in a room whose acoustics is a source of pleasure will reward you and motivate you to continue. We never play slow enough to get the full potential of pleasure that provides this instrument.

We can learn on our own. I am here to testify that it is possible. Of course, the result is not perfect, but unlike musicians who learn with academic guidelines in music conservatory, I continue to play after 10 years of practice and I still take pleasure on it !

Summary of the benefits of learning by yourself:

- No need for a thorough knowledge of solfege to be able to play an already rich baroque repertoire.

- No need for virtuosity in execution. You have to devote your energy to make the sound by taking your time. That's what gives pleasure.

The choice of the instrument

There is a common distinction between so-called "molded" body instruments and so-called "cut" body instruments. We are talking here about the way of elaboration of the soundboard and the back panel constituting the sounding board. The instruments of study, are made in factories of Central Europe or China which produce them in large quantity and export all over the world. The manufacturing of the instrument is such that the production time is minimized to gain on the manufacturing cost and the drying time of the wood. The table and the bottom are made from "boards" of spruce and maple which will be shaped by pressing and steaming to obtain the desired shape. The varnish is synthetic and the final appearance obtained without sanding. The cello of study is easily recognizable by the smooth and uniform aspect of the wood constituting the bottom and the ribs:

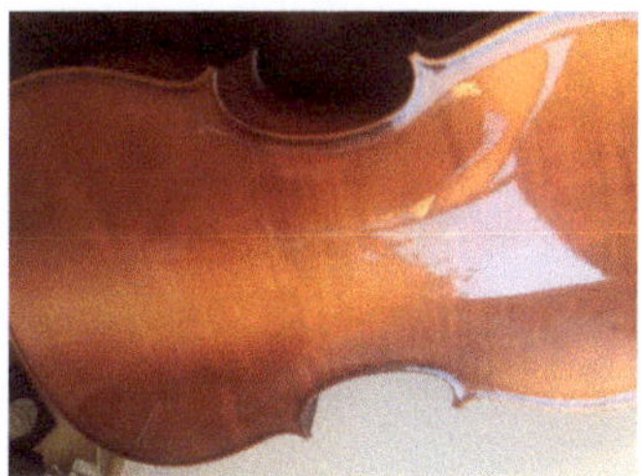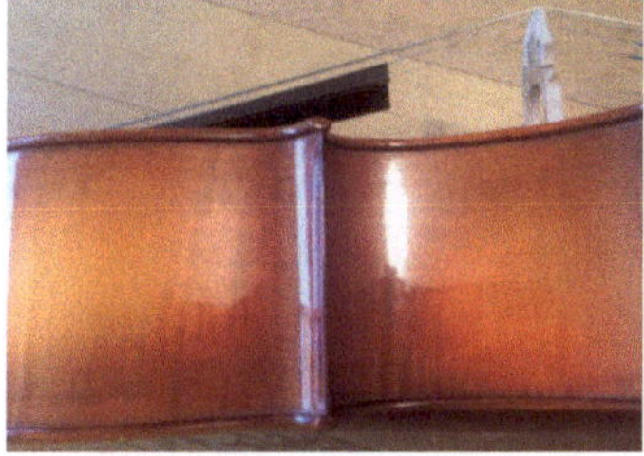

The instruments of professional players are made in Western Europe by instrument makers and in Eastern Europe and China by the same factories mentioned above. The ribs and the maple bottom, whose appearance is characterized by a kind of natural stripping dark and clear, are produced by "trimming" the plane of blocks of wood that have been previously dried five to ten years. Very often, this planning is obtained mechanically by a machine of duplication guided by a jig. The planning is done at the end of the cutting, to homogenize and to correct the thicknesses that vary between four and five millimeters, between the middle and the edges of the faces.

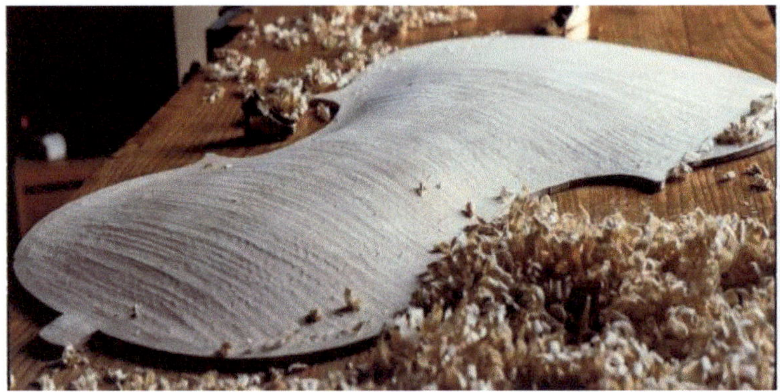

The varnish is oil based. It requires careful sanding between each layer. A finished instrument can have seven to ten layers, each of which has been sanded! The manufacturing duration of such an instrument requires at least three months of elaboration.

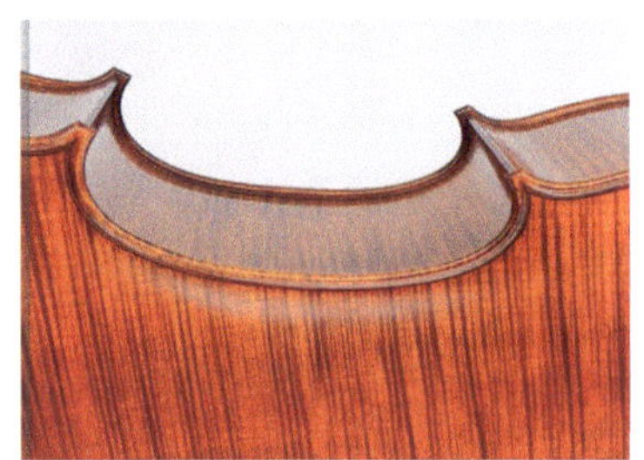 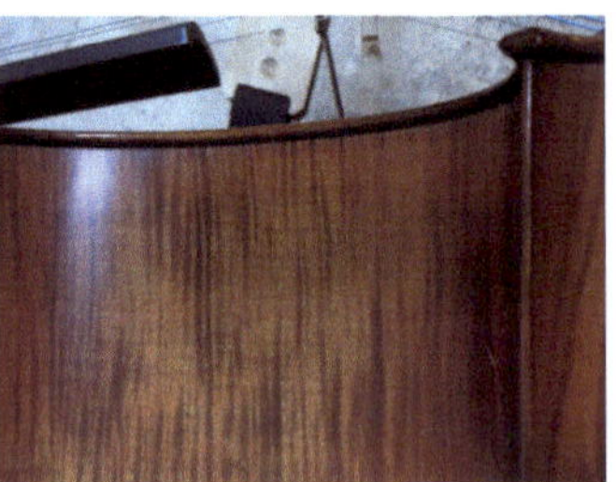

The sound box of a professional instrument will be lighter and drier than the one of a study instrument. This will result in a better fullness of the bass sounds, especially those produced from the fourth "G "string.

I personally acquired an instrument of this type after starting with a basic cello. I went to the GLIGA factory located in the Carpathians in Romania and visited it. I was able to observe the various stages of manufacturing and I could try several instruments before buying one. Frankly it's worth doing the trip and the visit, given the discount that the factory will give you, compared to the price charged in an instrument store. It's a matter of passion!

The instrument maker - his role

We must not confuse what is meant by instrument dealers and instrument makers, whether or not they have a shop or a website for selling on the internet. The instrument maker provides after-sales service, but more than that; that of adviser but also of "doctor" of your instrument which, over time, can see its stamp drifting unfavorably . I say voluntarily doctor because the instrument maker knows how to diagnose then to remedy, often free besides, with the problem which you are confronted .

It sounds bad, the tone is hoarse. This may be due to the relative position of the internal sound post in relation to the bridge. An adjustment is required.

The sound is really muffled and it sounds much less strong than before the holidays. The feet of the bridge do not perfectly fit the curve of the soundboard. It must be re-cut or replaced if it is already a little twisted by the pressure of the strings.

Impossible to play string III without rubbing on string II. This always happens on an attack. Is the upper part of the bridge not well shaped ? Maybe it needs to be re-cut? The interposition of a piece of parchment under string III can simply solve the problem

The sound post has fallen. Impossible to recover it in the sound box. It is necessary to know that the box of a new instrument is curved under the pressure exerted by the sound post. At the end of a year, it must be replaced by a longer one which will put again the sound box under strength.

My instrument was knocked during transport. I think it could be cracked.

It sounds too loud. My neighbors complain. How to reduce sound level without using a mute?

Here are some examples of problems that require the intervention of an instrument maker. I hope I convinced you? The other benefit of using an instrument maker is that he rents instruments for students at the music conservatory next door. if you do not want to get involved in purchasing an instrument, that may be a good solution. Check anyway that he has instruments of size 4/4 available, for adults.

The budget

If you hesitate and are not sure to get started for at least a year in learning this instrument. Adopt the rental solution.

 * Count a budget of **$ 25 to 35 per month for the instrument**. An amount of guarantee has to be paid at the beginning. Plan to insure it in order to cover the risks of theft or breakage.

* Purchase of **essential accessories: $ 150**

* **Course:** It should cost an amount from **$ 25 to 45 per lesson**. You would need **a minimum of 5 lessons for starting**.

Useful advise: it is better for you to have your teacher go to your home rather than the other way around, i.e. to his home or to a private music conservatory. The benefit will then be considered as home-based employment and thus with reduced tax. In practice, it will only come-back to you at half the price charged. Please check that it is applicable in your country.

Another advantage of this: rather than being confronted with his or her teaching habits that often aim to make you to take the maximum of lessons, you will be psychologically in a better position to ask him what you want to learn. This situation would be more profitable for you.

Some internet sites are specialized to find you a teacher who will go at your place. Please check in order to minimize costs of lessons. In the US, you would find the following companies who cover a numerous of the main cities of the country:

***Lessons in your home**,

***Teachers & Staff Music Opus 1**,

***Falcetti Music**,

***Henderson Academy of Music**.

Please check that they propose cello teachers because most of them only teach only piano and guitar.

Remember: **No additional lessons and method of solfege** should   be taken. Your memories of college should be sufficient.

If you are confident to get started, I advise you to start by **acquiring a cello study, from $ 450 to 1000** and later a cello semi-professional, to the extent that you have a room to play with good acoustic qualities.

Despite the enticing ads on the internet, do not start buying a very low cost instrument that can be found from $ 200 to 300.

Here are some price estimations for essential accessories:

*** cover: $ 40**   Even if you rent, you will probably be asked to buy a cover (see chapter 4 transport) and keep in mind that a protective shell for transport by airplane costs the same price as a semi-professional instrument. It is useless, even if you plan to move with your instrument, to engage in this sumptuary expenditure!

*** Rosin: $ 15**

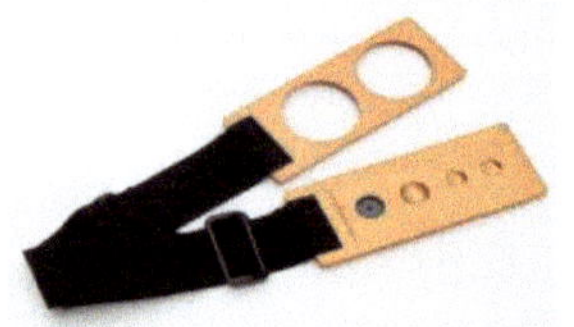

*** cello endpin rest: $ 20 to 35**

*** an electronic metronome: $ 15 to 40**

*** a set of strings: $ 120 to 250** . If you have to buy new strings even in the case of a rental, prefer, even to begin, strings of good quality and from well-known brand as LARSEN or JARGAR.

*** folding desk for the music scores: $ 20**

*** learning method**: - method of the young cellist: **$ 30**

*** bow: $ 70 to 200.**

*** acoustic tailpiece with 4 fine tuning knobs: $ 110**

*** instrument maker's performance** as a change of sound post or bridge or rework of a bow: **$ 130 to 150**

Time available - when to play?

Do not attempt to practice too much. In the beginning, do not spend more than half an hour studying a piece of music, excluding installation and warm-up time, which may take up to 15 minutes. After the acquisition of a certain ease in the execution you will be able to play from an hour to an hour and a half. This time can be spent playing two or three different pieces. Avoid polarizing yourself on the same piece for months while expecting perfection. You will tire your audience, your neighbors and in the end you will get tired yourself!

It is far better **to play in the morning**. You will find that this is when your body and your brain have the best ease and availability. Choose this period of the day to work on dexterity or decipher exercises or difficult pieces. The evening practice after work and a long time of transport is of course possible, if you cannot do otherwise. But prefer relaxation for this period by tackling only easy pieces of music that you have played many times. As soon as the game starts to get degraded by lack of attention, concentration or dexterity, stop playing and put away your instrument. Do not practice after the evening meal, especially if you have drunk alcohol. It is a paradox to note that concerts only take place in the evening and often at a late hour. This is all the more meritorious for musicians who are not at their best. You will see it yourself as you practice! To progress, it is better to play at least twice a week and about one hour or one hour and a half in the morning on weekends.

There is a distinctive sign to know if you play enough: a certain callosity of the pulp of your left fingers will be formed (caused by the pressing on the strings). You will maintain your level without progressing if you play only once a week. If you really want to take a significant step in your progress, you have to take lessons. In this case, plan for five to ten consecutive lessons at home.

For various practical reasons such as the space available for playing, the absence of noise annoyance of neighbors, It is necessary to avoid a practice which would be limited only to holiday periods. Because as for the practice of a foreign language in situ, you will spend the year to lose what you have learned during holidays.

The room where to play

Nobody talks about it but to give you an idea, please watch and listen videos of the Bach suites performed by great musicians. Unanimously, they chose a church as a showcase to enhance their game.

My opinion is that the place where you play is as important as the instrument itself for the quality of the sound. The cello is a sonorous instrument. If you practice in a small room, typically a room of 10 to 15 m2, you will have a saturation of the sound. As a consequence it will lead you when you play, to hold your right hand. Gradually you will adopt a defect that will prevent you from getting the fullness of your game.

I think that the mute, whether rubber or metal, is to proscribe. If you start playing with a mute, you will gain confidence in this practice that will become a hard habit to leave. Playing at a reduced sound level, reassures, especially when the accuracy and rhythm are lacking, which is normal at first. Your interaction with the environment, your family, your neighbors and yourself will certainly be limited. It will eventually encourage you in this practice of inhibition.

It must also be known that a new instrument, if it is perpetually restrained by a mute, will not develop over time the fullness of its timbre. I had this experience with a semi-professional instrument, sound powerful enough, that I clamped with a metal mute. After a few years, it became more and more hoarse and I even considered selling it as it became unpleasant to the ear. I had it modified for timbre improvement at an instrument maker and then used it only in a large room where its sound has gradually recovered, all its fullness.

What kind of room would be ideal for cello practice?

This is an opinion based on my own experience because I am not a specialist in acoustics. However, it seems to me that a rather rectangular room, of a minimum surface of the order of 30 m2 and especially with a **ceiling height , about 3.5 m to 5 m**, would give any satisfaction. The room must **produce a very slight reverberation**, which can be discerned by clapping in your hands.

A vaulted cellar can also do the trick. But You will have to heat it anyway.

The ability to play in an **acoustically satisfying room is almost for me, the most important factor** in deciding to learn to play the cello.

3 The basics of your learning

A bit of music theory - choice of scales and appropriate scores to begin

The clef of FA is the one that is by far the most common

you will notice it in cello scores: 

There are also cello scores of baroque music written in UT clef:

As a beginner, however, we will avoid using scores written in UT clef to avoid confusion in the learning of fingerings.

For any clef, there are major and minor scales. For our learning, we will retain only the following three most common scales with their coded notations:

- The scale of DO MAJOR 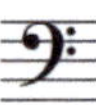

- The scale of SOL MAJOR 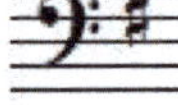

- The scale of FA MAJOR 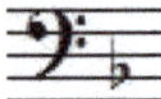

Just knowing that with a bit of practice , some music pieces in the following scales will be accessible to you:

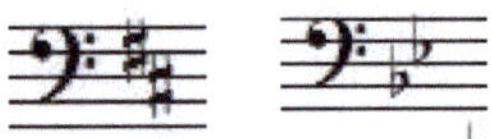

For the future, you do not need to know the name of these scales by heart. **Remember only their graphical notation.**

It is also not necessary to remember the name of the notes on the score and the note of each string played freely, i.e. without intervention of the left hand. The Anglo-Saxons designate the strings by I, II, III, IV or A, D, G, C. The string I or A is the treble one.

When you select the scores you want to play, remember only those written in FA clef and the three usual scales above.

Avoid annotated scores of the following symbols reserved for confirmed musicians:

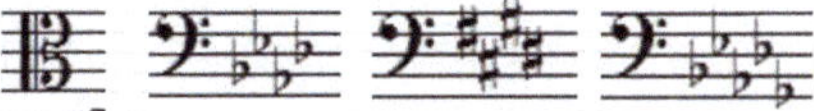

The notes whose accuracy is the easiest to obtain are on the one hand the « free » strings of course and on the other hand those resulting from the fingering of the left hand of called **the first position**. The highest position of the left hand is called the first position. You will therefore favor the playable partitions in first position..

This is viewable on the scores by the following range of notes:

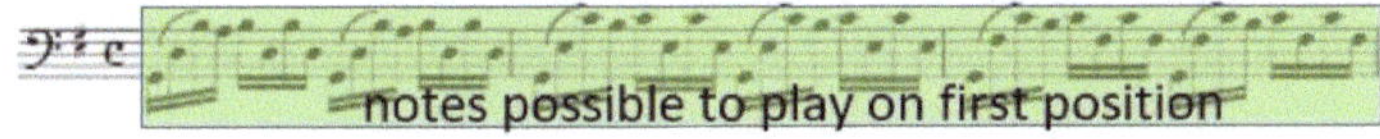

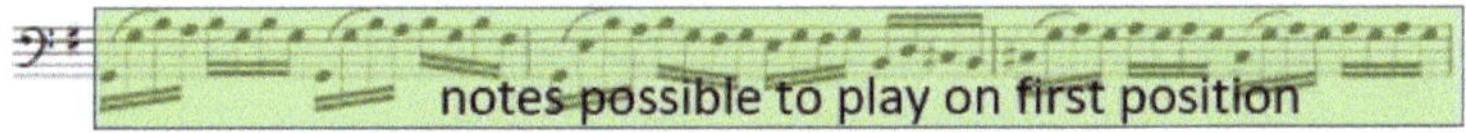

The difficulty of the game of the left hand comes with the very treble notes. For that, we will adopt other positions. We will have to position the left hand lower, closer and closer to the bridge depending on whether we are looking for more and more treble notes. This corresponds to the 2nd, 3rd, 4th position, etc. It is thus possible to play the cello in a very treble range, similar to that of the violin. But this requires great practice. Music scores to be rejected for a beginner contain ranges of treble notes that can be viewed as follows :

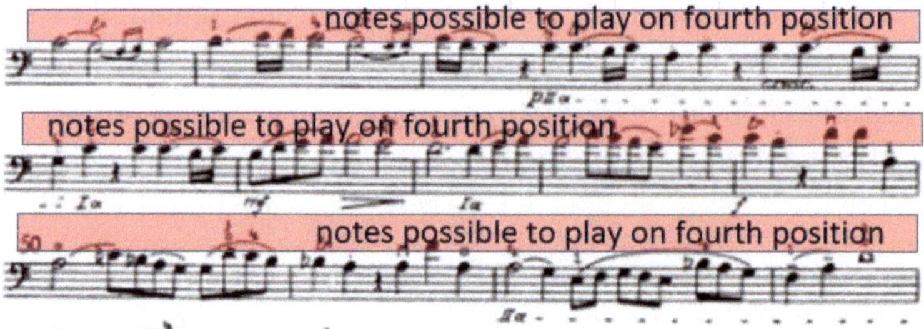

These landmarks should help you to quickly select which music score will be suitable for you and which ones require a confirmed musician practice.

So if you accept and apply these advises then you will be able to play the notes of « simple » scores. I propose now to associate with each note and for a given scale, the appropriate fingering.

A bit of music theory - the left hand and the fingering

This method is inspired by the one taught for the guitar. The fingerboard of the cello however does not include sills or marks, as on the neck of the guitar, which are pressed by the fingers of the left hand in order to obtain the rightness of the notes. There are two reasons for this.

The cellist looks mostly at his score or the conductor but never watches at his left hand playing. In the first position, it is also impossible to have a look at his fingers positioned almost at the cheek height !

The combination of positions and scales, sometimes including so-called « altered notes », would require to integrate in the fingerboard an almost infinity of sills, source of confusion rather than help for the musician.

For these two reasons, the cellist as well as the violinist uses fingerings. Each finger is automatically positioned at the desired position on the fingerboard.

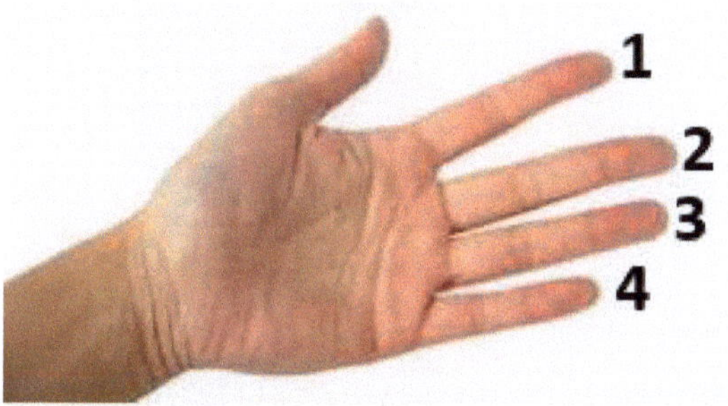

We first note the following convention of naming the fingers; namely "1" for the index, "2" for the middle finger, "3" for the ring finger and "4" for the little finger.

For each usual scale mentioned in the previous paragraph, it corresponds to a position of the fingers on the fingerboard for the left hand, in order to obtain the desired note.

Please take the scale of **DO MAJOR**. The position of the fingers on the strings I, II, III, IV, or A, D, C, G is illustrated on the following figure:

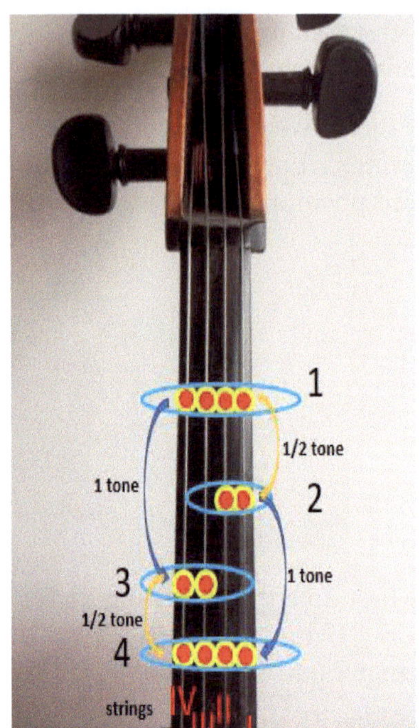

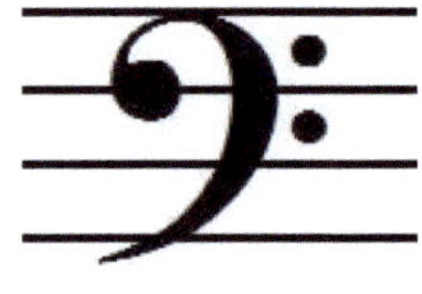

In fact to decline the full scale, we play in first position and for each string, first the string played freely, then three notes corresponding to the fingers (1, 2, 4) or (1, 3, 4). By illustrating the fingerings on the score this gives:

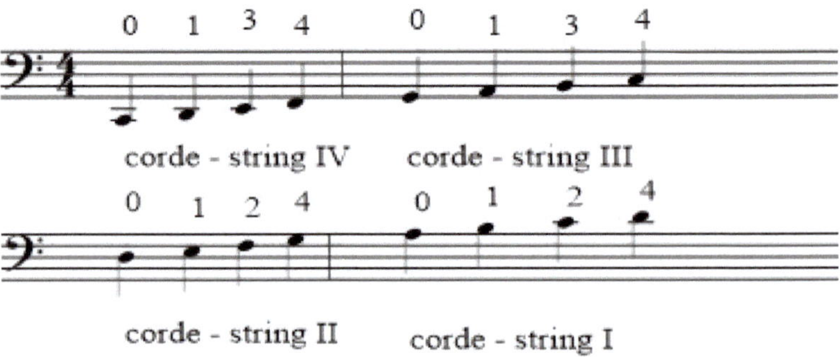

The fingering of the **SOL MAJOR** scale is slightly different from the previous scale about strings II and IV:

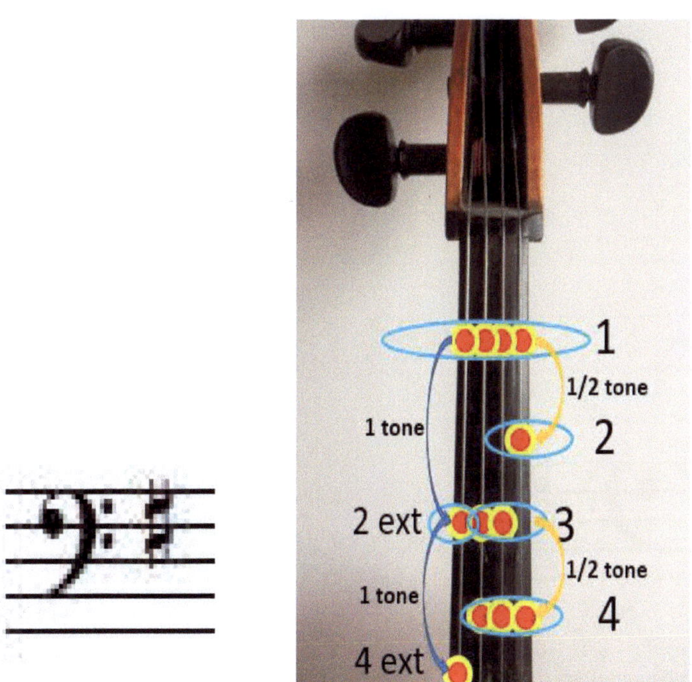

The fingerings on each string should be as followed:

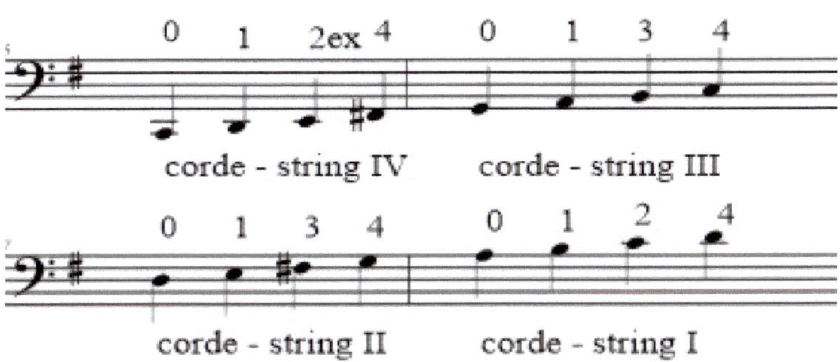

The fingering of the **FA MAJOR** scale is:

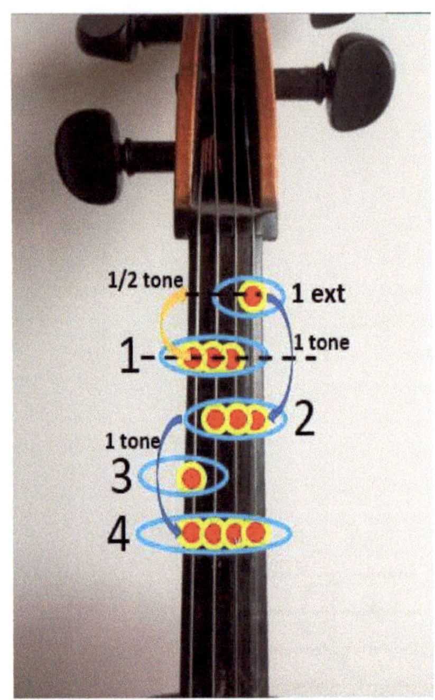

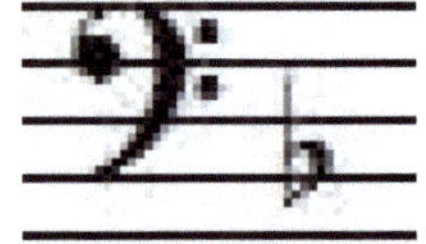

The fingerings on each string should be as followed:

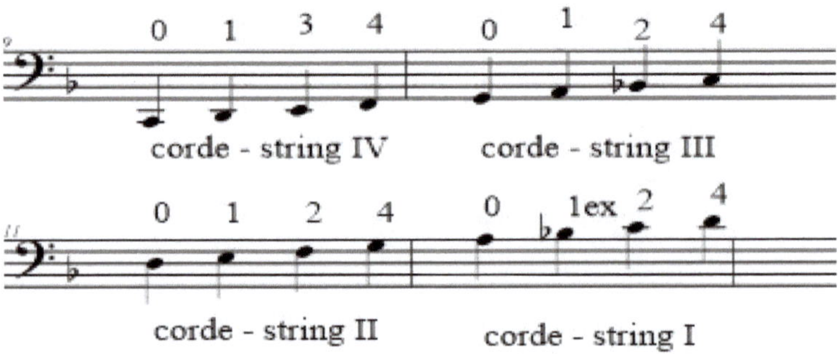

You have to work the spacing between the fingers to get and consolidate accuracy. I recommend at first to exercise your fingers with a method, with which you can listen and play the notes simultaneously (see 2, the Method of Young Cellist Michel Tournus including a CD of recorded scores) and with a teacher in a second time.

This paragraph is the most important to assimilate for learning your instrument.

As you find the rightness of the notes when playing, do not hesitate to **mark the fingerings with stickers** to stick on the fingerboard:

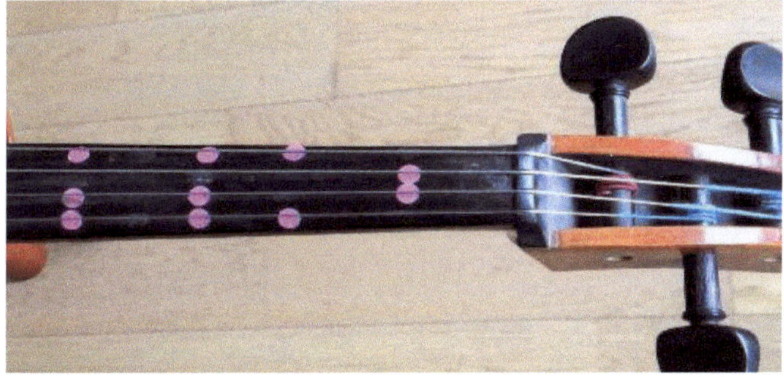

Please learn and work only one scale at a time!

Summary on learning scales and fingerings:

- Restrict yourself when choosing or acquiring the scores with which you will start. Start with simplest ones, the three most common scales and the first position.

- No one needs for practicing to know the name of the notes, nor complex notions of solfege like the succession of whole notes, altered, etc ... Only the visual recognition of the scales

and the correspondence between the notes and the fingering are important .

- Do not hesitate to stick stickers on the fingerboard of your instrument to serve as a landmark. Only work in one scale at a time.

- Work on the accuracy of the fingerings, that is to say the distance between the position of the fingers of the left hand with a method which includes the sound production at first, then with a teacher in a second time

A bit of music theory - the movement of the bow and the rhythm

The rhythm is significantly more difficult to acquire than the note accuracy. We think we can solve the problem by using a metronome. This is only partly true. The metronome allows you to maintain the right tempo, from the beginning until the end of the song. The natural tendency is to accelerate imperceptibly. If you already have a few months of practice, you can now work the movement of the right hand, which will allow you to master the rhythm within each measure.

We must consider two rhythms. The general rhythm is the tempo of the melody. This is the pulsation that will give the metronome, which goes from slow (Largo, then Moderato) through (Andante) and growing up (Allegro). This is not the most difficult point to work.

The "local" rhythm consists in respecting the relative duration of each note within each measure. This is the difficulty.

There are "rules" that your teacher will teach you. But know it, none is applicable in all situations. They must often be combined.

The right hand controls the rhythm. We will try to make as regular as possible the relative movement of the bow, like a pendulum, from the left to the right, then from the right to the left. We can also practice without involving the left hand and fingering, to work the regularity of the movement of the bow.

The scores sometimes mention some symbols which correspond to the bow movement to start with :

The symbol ⊓ means to **pull** the bow and respectively the symbol V means to **push**.

Notes linked together to be played in the same bow stroke are noted as follows:

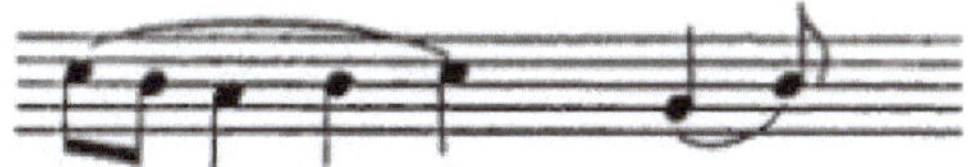

Rule n ° 1:

It is necessary, in order to keep a good rhythm, to play with a regular rocking movement of the bow from left to right then from right to left, ensuring each time a complete stroke, from the guard to the end. We can use the landmark that constitutes the length of the bow. So to play the notes:

* one round note = 4 beats = 1 full bow length

* a white dotted note = 3 beats = ¾ of bow length

* a white note ♩ = 2 beats = ½ of bow length

* a black note ♩ = 1 beat = ¼ bow length, ...

However, we can hardly go any further in the execution of notes taken individually, by giving them a portion of bow length for notes of very small duration as for, triplets ... Hence the obvious limitations of this method which only works when there is on the scope, a relative homogeneity of duration of the notes and groups of notes linked together. For example ,white with black, etc ...

This rule is however particularly suitable for playing a succession of arpeggios or a combination of arpeggios and isolated notes as follows:

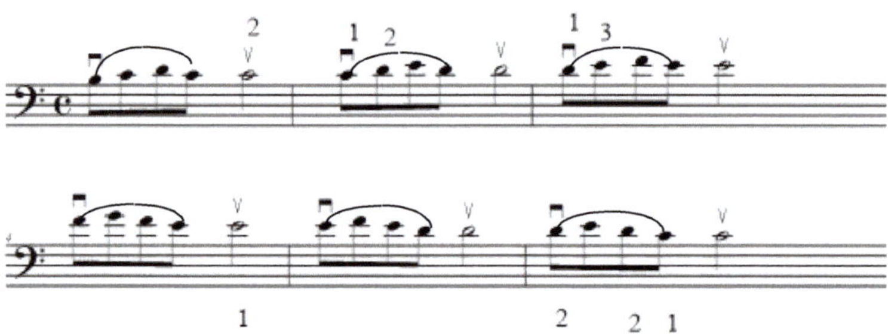

In this example, the measure contains 4 beats. Within each measure we will play the 4 linked notes in a bow stroke while pulling, then the white note in a bow stroke while pushing. Thus each stroke of bow will be 2 beats and its speed and its stroke will be the same in each direction. So you can manage without the metronome here!

Rule n ° 2:

For musical reasons, that is to say, to better highlight the attacks and to print personality to your game, it is often better to begin the bow movement by pulling. We play in fact stronger by pulling than by pushing.

The duration of the measure is constant throughout the piece it is therefore necessary to manage to divide each measure in bow strokes so as to be in the position to pull at the beginning of the next measure. The application of this rule is obviously easier for an even number of beats in the measure.

Exception: Sometimes, however, the song starts with an incomplete measure. In this case, we will always begin the piece by pushing the bow

In the following example, the measure has 3 beats, which is an odd number of beats.

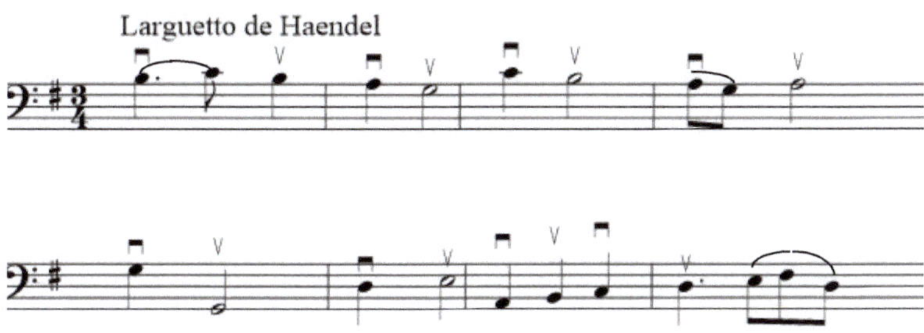

We will assign 2 beats for the movement of the bow stroke from left to right, then 1 beat for the movement of the bow stroke from right to left. The speed of the bow will be then different. However, the movement back and forth of the bow will be identical from one measure to another.

There is, however, a clear break in the movement of the bow by applying Rule No. 2, between the 3rd and 4th measure of the 2nd line. In the 3rd measure, we will play each black with a full bow movement then the 4 linked notes of the 4th measure with a single bow movement.

This last situation, from the moment when the bow movement no longer allows you to correctly chant the rhythm, can admit a compromise, that is to say another cut of the bow strokes in a measure. Divide them according to your best ability to play the sequence of the notes. Take your freedom too!

Summary on Learning Rhythm and the Right Hand:

- Do not work the rhythm until you have already acquired a certain ease of accuracy. Starting your learning by simultaneously working both things, may require a concentration and coordination of actions, too important. This may discourage you and therefore incites you to give up.

- It is not the metronome that will help you the most in order to play rhythmically but the regular movement of the bow you will acquire. Please practice first playing the bow with the left hand free, as regularly as possible and with the same beat.

- Analyze the score you learn. Then identify for this one the rule that would apply best. If necessary, annotate the score by writing the appropriate bow strokes (pull, push) with the proper symbols.

- A relative control of the rhythm is essential to play in group with other musicians.

The lessons to start

To get started effectively in your self -learning, it is necessary to take some preliminary lessons. But for them to be profitable, you must be precise or even directive towards your music teacher about what you want to work. Starting lessons with great beginners is not common. It is therefore essential to prepare the ground so that he does not improvise and that he doesn't engage in reflexes of academic type of teaching, in excess of duration but without real added value. It's really not useful and it's wasted money that a teacher to be there to watch your rhythm or bow exercises for hours.

It is therefore necessary to anticipate the lessons and to solicit the teacher only to acquire the essential bases for the continuation of your learning in an autonomous way. What are they ?

Before meeting your teacher, **you must collect the instrument, accessories, a method** (L. L. FEUILLARD for example) **and stickers.**

The first five lessons can be organized according to the following learnings:

1) learn the position, the holding of the bow and the movements of the bow by working the unrolling of the right arm during regular movements by pushing and pulling.

 2) **acquire the fingering of the DO MAJOR range**. Have your cello tuned first, then place properly the stickers **for all the strings** with your teacher (fingerings in the first position) corresponding to this scale. Practice going down this scale from the fingering 4 of the string I or A. After the lesson and by yourself, practice raising the scale from the IV or G string « free » until the first string or A string on the 4th fingering.

 3) **go up and down the scale of DO MAJOR by working** the accuracy and **regularity of the bow movement**. Complete bow course by working the regularity of speed and wrist force applied on bow.

4) Begin lessons 1 and 2 of L.R. FEUILLARD method. To **get started, learn to read a score. You will play annotating the fingering of all notes** in pencil focusing on accuracy and fingering.

Take 2-3 weeks to work on your own lessons 1,2,3 up to and including 5 of the Feuillard method.

5) book the 5th and final lesson to check with your teacher the consolidation of your lessons 1 to 5. Not too long, so start lesson 6! **Start learning related notes and linking notes of varying duration (black and white).**

Check that you are able to work on your own lessons 6, 7 and 8. Give yourself 2 months for this. If you cannot, sign up for 5 more lessons

---

Summary of what you need to prepare to optimize your lessons:

- Before taking your lessons, make sure your material is available and ready: tuned cello, accessories, method and stickers.

- Lead your teacher on the essentials topics you feel you need to acquire such as position, holding the bow and the movement of the right arm, the fingering of the scale of DO Major with the stickers on the fingerboard. Everything else is to be considered optional.

- NO THEORY OF SOLFEGE. You do not need it.

---

4 The practice

The position

At first you should keep in mind that the position to adopt is your position and not the one that your teacher would impose on you, which, moreover, will vary according to the teacher. It takes several months to find your ideal position. It must be natural. In fact the only adjustment is the length of the endpin you will deploy

First you have to set the top position of the instrument in relation to you. By lifting the neck of the cello slightly, the lower right peg position should coincide with your ear. It remains now to adjust the inclination of the sound box with the deployment of the endpin. It is in a way the « potentiometer » of the sound level of the instrument.

If the endpin is fully deployed, please try it, this will bring the body of the instrument closer to you and in particular the bridge. The soundboard of the instrument will be more horizontal. Some musicians like Tortelier adopted an endpin bent down to accentuate this effect. Mechanically, this position leads on the one hand to increase the pressure that the arm will exert on the bow and to bring the bridge closer to your right wrist for the attack of the strings on the other hand. The bow will be naturally positioned near the bridge (about 5 cm). You will find that this setting will make you play harder as long as that you are able to maintain the force on the bow according to your need. This position is the most tiring. In addition to the support of the right arm, it requires to raise the left elbow strongly to be able to perform fingerings of the first position. This is the setting usually adopted by professional musicians when playing solo because they play more often in alternative positions than the first one.

If the endpin is moderately extended (about 25 to 30 cm), the body of the instrument moves away from you and your bow will naturally position itself at a greater distance from the bridge for the attack of the strings (of the order of 10 cm). The effort needed to produce a harmonious sound is less. You will also play less hard. You will also have less need to lift the left elbow. And your right arm will be less bent. This position is less tiring than the previous one. It's up to you to choose what suits you best.

To know how to install the strings and to tune his instrument

The cello has four strings tuned in fifths: DO, SOL, RE and LA (from bass to treble tone). In English they are called C, G , D ,A. It is for this simple reason that the technique explained later and that I recommend to you, is called the tune in fifths (as opposed to the practice of the direct tune with an electronic buzzer). For information, the cello is tuned an octave below the viola and respectively an octave plus a tune in fifths below the violin. This is one of the instruments which is able of the largest tonal range. It is important to know how to tune your instrument. However, it must be kept in mind that a cello is very stable and can remain well tuned for years, if it is not used, except the treble « A » string that will gradually distend to a less treble tone. I do not advise on the purchase of an electronic tuner as do for example the guitarists. The sound emitted by a cello subjected to a bow is very rich and composed of many harmonics. It looks nothing like the one emitted by an electronic buzzer. In practice, you may not be able to associate with the ear, the LA or « A » of the buzzer and the LA or « A » of the cello. So I propose the following guideline based on the tune in fifths which means practically to play the strings two per two while searching the most harmonious sound.

First you have to determine a landmark which will correspond to the harmonic position on the fingerboard. From a cello already tuned, you will perform this step BEFORE disassembling the strings, especially for transport. Take your instrument, lay it flat on your knees and pinching the strings, starting with the bass or « C » string, then find where is the harmonic position. Proceed as follows: The zone is at the connection elbow between the body and the neck. Play first with the finger, the string free, then before the extinction of the sound put your finger on the string, without pressing and listen to the resulting sound. The harmonic is clearly heard when you find the exact position. This position on the fingerboard is the same for all strings. Check it. Once this position is found, **mark it with a white paint on the fingerboard. This mark is extremely useful** for tuning and also for playing. It will serve you very frequently.

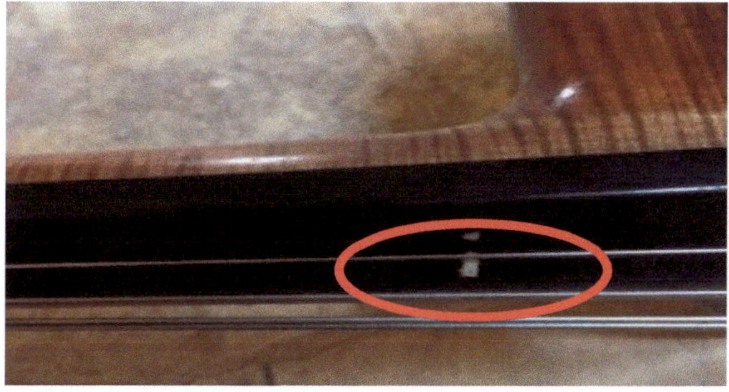

Then, whenever necessary, proceed to the tuning of the instrument. Once all the strings and the bridge are mounted and positioned correctly, tune the instrument starting with the bass string whose sound you have previously memorized, by ear, including playing the string and the following three notes corresponding to the fingering 1,3,4. It is important to tune the first string ensuring that the three other strings are already mounted and stretched. Because the tension of the other strings affects the tune of the string you are setting.

Now move on to tune the following strings: Put your cello flat on your lap and play freely the next string. Compare the sound obtained with the bass string on which you pressed the finger at the position of the harmonic that you already marked in the previous step. The sound must be identical. If the sound of the second string is too low, then stretch the string by turning the appropriate peg. Conversely if the sound is too high, adjust the peg in order to reduce the stretch until finding the correct tone. the same with the third string and so on. Be careful the « A » string is fragile and you must not stretch it too much!

Once a first approximate tune has been reached, fine tuning is required. You will then adjust the tone of the strings with accuracy using the fine tune knobs on the tailpiece. Please check first that you keep enough clearance to screw the fine tune knobs.

Hold your instrument as if to play and use your bow. Start by playing together the A and D strings. The sound obtained must be harmonious and pleasant to hear. In any case not nasal. The reason for this is that the difference in tune between two consecutive strings played freely is a tune in fifths, so nearly a chord. So we have to get mutual tuning between these two consecutive strings. If it is not good, adjust the tension of the high string with the fine tune located on the tailpiece. Start by stretching slightly. Try with the bow. The sound obtained with both strings must improve. If this is the case, continue the tension until you get the harmonious sound. If your sound deteriorates, do the opposite and relax the string.

Check that your stickers are well positioned:

Play the string I or « A » (the treble one) and put the fourth finger on the fingerboard at its proper location. Is it right ? If not, look for the right string further down the key. When you think you have found it, play the string « A » on the fourth finger and the string « D » free at the same time. It must sound harmoniously. If this is not the case, go back slightly and start over. To play fair, your fourth finger must now be at the exact position on the fingerboard. In this step, you must never adjust the accuracy with the pegs near the scroll ! you will lose all the settings and spend some time to find the fine tuning of your instrument!

The explanation is that between two musical sessions, the tune of string « A » could slightly deviate. The other strings in principle should remain at the correct tension.

Once this fine adjustment is obtained, proceed by the same way by tuning the second string while simultaneously playing the second and the third string. And so on. Always start with the treble string because the chord to the tune in fifths of the bass strings is insensitive and difficult to discern in the ear.

This tuning phase playing all the range also serves you to calibrate the gap between your finger positions on the fingerboard.

The ultimate check is to be made by playing the full range with the bow successively on the four strings with all the fingerings. If this is unsatisfactory, fine tuning must be started again, beginning with the alleged string that is false. Repeat to play the string to the tune in fifths of the other strings. Then play a piece that you know quite well. If it's ok, your instrument is tuned. From an instrument completely disassembled, the tune of the instrument will take you from half an hour to one hour. Concentrate on this essential prerequisite and do not try to play later. You will postpone this to the next day. Obviously doing such like this is infinitely longer than a teacher or a music instrument maker will practice. This reflects the difference of ear between a professional and a beginner!

Summary of how to tune a cello with a tune in fifths:

- No need for an electronic buzzer.

- Locate and mark the position of the harmonics on the fingerboard,

- Roughly adjust the tension of the strings by acting on the pegs and starting with the bass by plucking the strings (as on the guitar), instrument flat on your knees,

- Perform the fine tuning by playing the strings with the bow in pairs. Look for the harmonious sound that matches the tune in fifths. The fine adjustment of the tension of the strings is made with the help of the fine tune knobs on the tailpiece.

- Check and start fine tuning with the fine tune knobs, if necessary. Never go back to peg adjustment !

Downloadable scores and accompanying sound

It is recalled here that downloading free sheet music is an infringement of the law on intellectual property and copyrights. We recall here the legislation:

Reprography of an edited score is prohibited. However, in some cases, conventions allow it. For example, use in the context of national education.

Nevertheless the extraction and the copy of a score is lawful in the case of a private use:

Photocopying of musical scores is not permitted by law except for the private use of the copyist (at the copyist's home) and for personal use. Reproductions made by individuals in the privacy of their home are covered. There is a website that overcomes the problem of obtaining free sheet music. It is a community of musicians who make adaptations of works by creating their own arrangements. These musicians share them free with the community, that is to say you can collect them if you are registered on the site. Registration is of course free. You can later suggest your own arrangement of a work with its associated score. The website is called MUSESCORE

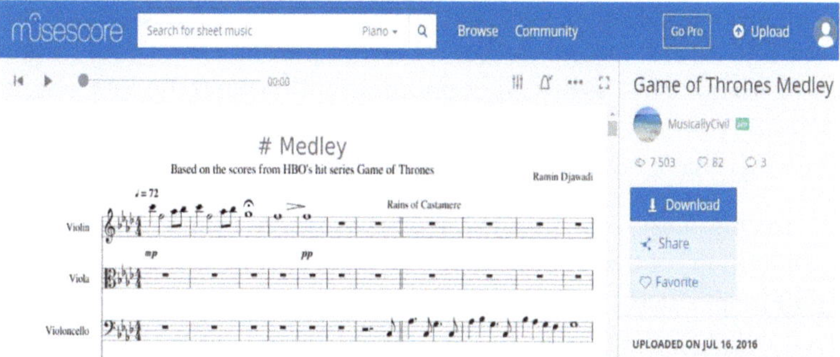

In this example, you can download the complete score or score by instrument in PDF format as well as the melody generated by a synthesizer in MP3 format. The sound is a little "chemical" nevertheless!

When playing the melody by the computer, the application visualizes its progress among the score, which allows you to identify difficulties.

Warning ! : Without knowing the reason, you should be aware that many websites that praise the free download of music scores are a significant source of computer viruses! Be careful and download only on recommended sites. Ask your teacher

How to carry your instrument ?

This is a problem that repels or even discourages the practice of an instrument considered bulky. The vision of these young musicians carrying their instrument on their backs in a rigid shell is not without reminding the character of Obélix delivering his menhir. It is rare to observe an adult musician moving such that way.

Personally I do not recommend the purchase of a rigid transport shell, also very expensive because its need does not seem justified. I rather recommend the purchase of a cover lined with foam. This lightweight padding will protect the instrument against minor shocks. Indeed, consider the situations for which you will have to carry your instrument :

- Taking lessons with a teacher: If you live in the countryside, you will drive there safely without any risk of damage. The cello will be perfectly protected in its cover.

If you live in a big city, you stay at home because it is the teacher who will move to your home and not the other way around (see chapter: Start learning - lessons),

- Playing in a group with other musicians: If you want to play in a group to socialize, prefer transport by car to the place of rehearsal. Personally, I carried my cello in the subway, protected in its cover. It is acceptable during off-peak hours.

If you play in a group to progress, here too modern techniques allow you to have the orchestra at home and therefore avoid moving (see chapter: technological developments at the service of learning)

- You are transferred in province or abroad: You necessarily go there by plane with your instrument.

For information: be aware that professional musicians who travel by plane buy two seats; one for them and the other for the instrument. In practice, the flight crew considers that the instrument placed on a seat, with or without a protective shell, is not properly secured. The hostess will place it in a cupboard.

  You are not professional and therefore how to proceed at lower cost? I personally practiced about 10 times the following method:

o Dismantle everything that makes the instrument cumbersome and fragile i.e. strings, pegs , bridge and tailpiece. It is very important in this operation to identify the position of the pegs which are tapered and paired in their respective dwellings.

o The instrument thus dismounted, put in its carrying cover, seems less bulky. If necessary, strap the cover around the neck and the scroll.

o When registering your luggage at the check in board, argue that you are moving with a kind of big guitar. It is imperative that your cello be recorded in "cabin baggage"

and that it be provided with an ad-hoc label that you will keep for the next trip.

o If you are traveling on a small plane, entrust your cello, like other passengers with their cabin suitcases, to the flight attendants, who will carefully put them in the aft cargo bay and put them on top of the rest. After landing you will immediately get your instrument down the bridge.

o Once you arrive at your destination, it will give you the opportunity to put into practice the precepts of stringing and tuning your instrument.

Important: any cello "protected" in a rigid protective shell and entrusted to the registration as checked baggage will be broken upon arrival. It happened to me ...

Summary of how to protect your instrument for transporting it:

- Do not buy a protective shell, prefer a cover.

- Do not panic about transporting your instrument by plane,

- For that, disassemble everything that makes it cumbersome and fragile; strings , pegs, bridge and cinch the cover around the neck and the scroll to minimize its volume,

- Register your instrument as a "cabin baggage".

- Take care before disassembling the pegs to locate their positions. They are paired.

How to organize your musical meeting

Whether you are starting out or have a few years of practice, your music session will always be organized in the same way:

* first correct the possible tuning deviation of your instrument,

* play the scale to adjust the fingering of your left hand and play the notes automatically,

To continue, play down and up the notes on all strings. Do this exercise, just playing. Your left hand, which you do not watch when you play, must take its position marks automatically. Replay the scale by looking ahead until you will play right.

This is why when you are very beginner, it is better to remain on the same scale, because your left hand acquires only one setting at a time.

* play your favorite music piece of the moment to warm up but also to gauge your form and your aptitude and availability,

* practice the two or three pieces you are studying, to confirm your ability

Finally, decipher your next piece.

During these different stages you will evaluate for yourself of your form. During the warm-up, if you make mistakes and are not happy with your game, stop and put away your instrument. Then, **don't forget to analyze very carefully why your game was bad.**

- You were concerned and confess it, you thought of something else and it distracted you,

- You had an exhausting day. You thought to relax by doing some music. But the form is not there,

- You have not played for a long time, the dexterity is no longer at the rendezvous. You need to practice more regularly,

- It's been several times since your instrument sounds bad. Frankly, I am convinced that it is wrong.

If you admit the reason you played badly, you will definitely progress! In a context of academic teaching, it is the guilt that comes from the bullying and the lack of self-analysis of your game that cause to give up .

Play your usual pieces of music trying to impose to yourself a very slow rhythm in order to work the accuracy of the sound and the rhythm. Then replay your piece by imposing the correct movement of the bow (attack the measure by pulling). When you play several consecutive measures, you must make sure, that each measure starts with the bow pulled (if applicable of course). In this exercise, play only one line of the music score and attack the second only if the result on the first line is positive. Finally, play in rhythm with the metronome, always very slowly.

I suggest you play three times each piece. At the third or even second, your game must be significantly better than the first time. If so, go ahead to decipher a new piece.

Decipher a new piece

Before embarking on the study of a new piece of music, it must be borne in mind that there have always been two ways of doing things. The one used by ear, that is to say by the repeated listening, then the reproduction step by step with the assistance of our auditory memory, the musical phrases constitutive of the melody. Either academic by proceeding with the reading and analysis of the score and then its simultaneous execution, scrupulously respecting the rules of solfege.

Listening and memorizing then playing without partition are practiced by the Gypsies ... but also by virtuosos soloists. It is this technique that gives the game the best virtuosity because thus, the time saved in reading the notes, can be used to fully devote to the game. It is known that it is impossible to play the 21 Caprices of Paganini, one of the major difficulties of the violin, by reading a score. Simply by limiting oneself to exclusive "ear" learning, one will soon find oneself limited with respect to the variety and duration of the pieces that make up one's own repertoire. It will also be difficult to play with other musicians, if one can not materialize on a score, the points on which it is necessary to work in concert.

Anyway I suggest you to learn by heart an easy and also very well-known pièce of cello which is the first « Bourrée of Bach Third Suite » :

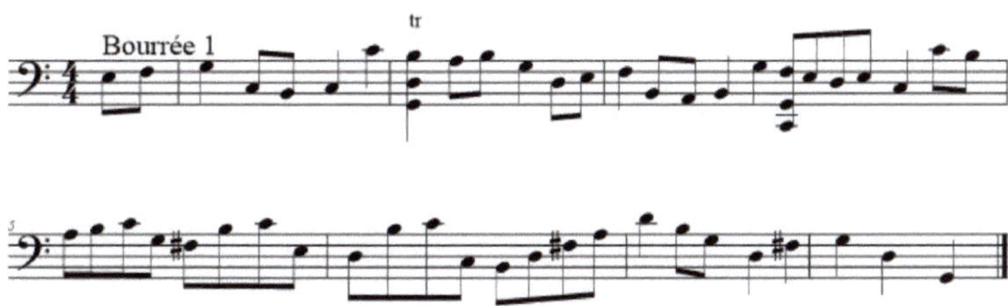

I noticed on my side, that working new pieces by decrypting partitions systematically, involves a kind of habits. You will find after a while that it will be very difficult for you to learn a new piece "by ear" and with the only help of your memory.

The best compromise for me, is to adopt a mixed practice taking into account that the rhythm and "phrasing" of a melody are the most difficult points to acquire. Work on accuracy and fingering with a music score. Bring a recording of the piece you are learning and play tirelessly in your car by singing it out loud during your daily travels. After one month, you will know by heart the beat and the phrasing. You will play the piece of music correctly.

If you are very beginner, do not worry about rhythm and bow movements at the moment. Concentrate on the accuracy of notes and accuracy of your game.

Start by annotating your score in pencil, mentioning the fingering corresponding to **each note**. For each music session, please work not much than two lines.

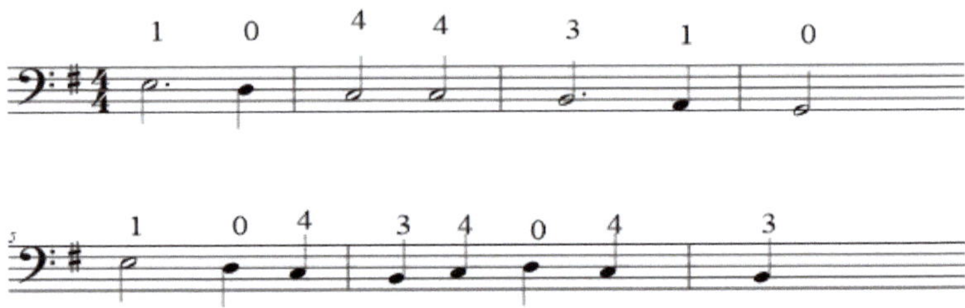

Locate the alterations, that is to say:

* The notes marked "   " have to be played ½ tone above the normal note. It will be necessary to shift the fingering of ½ tone towards the bottom of the fingerboard. For example if the normal note is played with the fingering "2", this altered note will be played with the fingering "3".

* On the contrary, the notes marked " " have to be played ½ tone below the normal note. It will usually be necessary to shift the hand of ½ tone to the top of the fingerboard,

The altered notes keep their alteration on at least one complete measure, that is to say between two vertical bars dividing the measure. The return to the normal note is indicated by the symbol " ":

To verify by ear that your annotation is correct, I invite you to recover the song that you decipher on YOUTUBE and to listen to it several times by following the melody on the score. When a note seems abnormal to your ear, it is probably an alteration. Then look for this note the appropriate fingering. Correct the fingering on the score accordingly. Again, do not worry about the accuracy of your game. It will come quickly.

If you already have a few months of practice and you feel that the correctness is acquired on the three usual scales, then you have to work the rhythm and the movement of the right hand. This task is significantly more difficult than the work of accuracy. So spend ½ hour and reduce your decryption not more than a line of score each time.

There is, as we have seen, a direct correspondence between the movement of your bow and the rhythm of your game. On some scores, the bow strokes are already mentioned by the symbol which means to pull the bow and respectively the symbol V which means to push. It can already be noted on the scope:

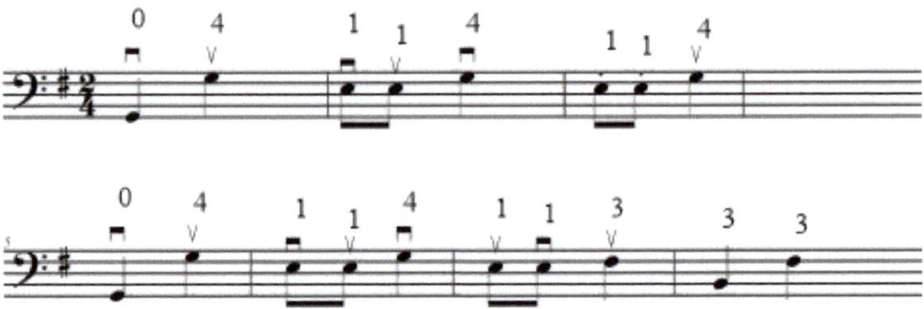

If this is not the case, annotate the bow movements for each measure on the score with the proper symbols, by referring to the appropriate rule to adopt. Do it in pencil because this work is difficult and gives rise to many iterations.

Play as slowly as possible by not trying to hang on to the melody. Refer for the bow movements to the indications in paragraph 3. Repeat the sequences where you hesitate and not the one you know.

Summary of how to decipher a new piece:

- *To do only when you warmed up and your game is correct.*

- *Annotate all notes in the score with the corresponding fingering. Be aware of alterations.*

- *When you are a little more experienced, annotate all bow movements on the score. Consider notes which should be played linked together in the same bow stroke.*

- *Limit yourself from one to a half line of score. Repeat your game only where you're stumbling.*

- Play as slowly as possible and emphasize the quality of the sound and the regularity of the movement of the bow.

---

4 Evolution of your practice

Playing in a group

Unmistakably as you progress, you will feel the urge to play in a group. You've noticed that practicing a two-voices piece of music with your teacher or a cellist friend is extremely rewarding, compared to playing with one voice. So you are looking for other musicians and you are tempted to push the door of a conservatory.

The latter will unfortunately accept you, besides the high registration fees, only if you have the viaticum, that is to say the years of solfege that you did not want to face. So you are stuck! Indeed, the difference you will have with other musicians is neither more nor less than five years of solfege !

Also, I advise you to stay on two-voices scores. As you are not yet in 4th position, study the accompaniment voice and practice with a partner who will play the main voice. So you will progress significantly in the rhythm.

If you still cannot synchronize with your partner, **I propose a solution where a virtual partner will accompany you**. For that it will adapt to your rhythm and will compensate your possible hesitations.

Technological evolutions at the service of learning

Fortunately, researchers at IRCAM (Research Institute of Music in France founded by Pierre Boulez) have looked into this problem and have worked to develop a musical accompaniment software tool for beginners:

« The results of IRCAM's recent research make it possible to overcome the problem of accompanying a beginner musician. An amateur musician may in fact want for practical reasons, to train and play his part alone, in the absence of other musicians. For that, it suffices, from the musical score, to delegate the parts of the other instruments to prerecorded sounds or to instrument synthesizers. In other words, the accompanying part can be replaced by a digital medium. In a fixed diagram, the accompaniment can be a simple sound recording (without the solo part). In this case, the solo part is executed synchronously with this fixed medium. In an ideal scheme, like a human musical accompaniment, **it is preferable for the accompaniment of beginners, that it is the part of accompaniment which adapts in real time to the play of the instrumentalist**: to slow down or accelerate the speed of interpretation, and modify the dynamics according to the interpretation of the work. In this case, we need an automatic accompaniment system.

In automatic accompaniment, the computer plays the role of a virtual musician and acts according to the playing of the instrumentalist in real time. It must therefore be equipped with a real-time listening capacity as well as an ability to undertake musical actions in coordination and synchronously with the playing of the instrumentalist. It thus takes as input the solo score as well as the accompaniment score, and uses the flow of sound in real time to listen, synchronize and react according to the musical text. The overall pattern of event scheduling remains the same, but the temporal proportion of events and their internal relationships fluctuate during the performance of the musician and his performance. While listening, it is also obvious that the accompaniment acts according to the game in real time: it slows down and in this case waits the interpreter during breaks. The other essential point, comparing the two interpretations, is the presence of possible errors on the part of our amateur musician. Despite the errors, the system must be able to musically manage the accompaniment and not necessarily stop, which is the case in the middle of this interpretation. » How to proceed to dispose of this tool?

The brand **ANTESCOFO** whose developers come from IRCAM was created in 2016 in Paris. An application on smartphone, called **METRONAUT** has been developed. This app is free and available on APPLE-STORE. Today there are only 4 works available in the cello repertoire. However, this application progresses and will expand very quickly.

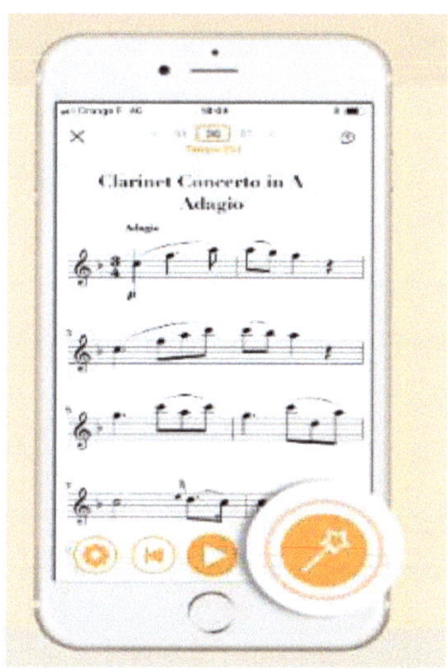

Fingering of other scales suggested

Si bemol major

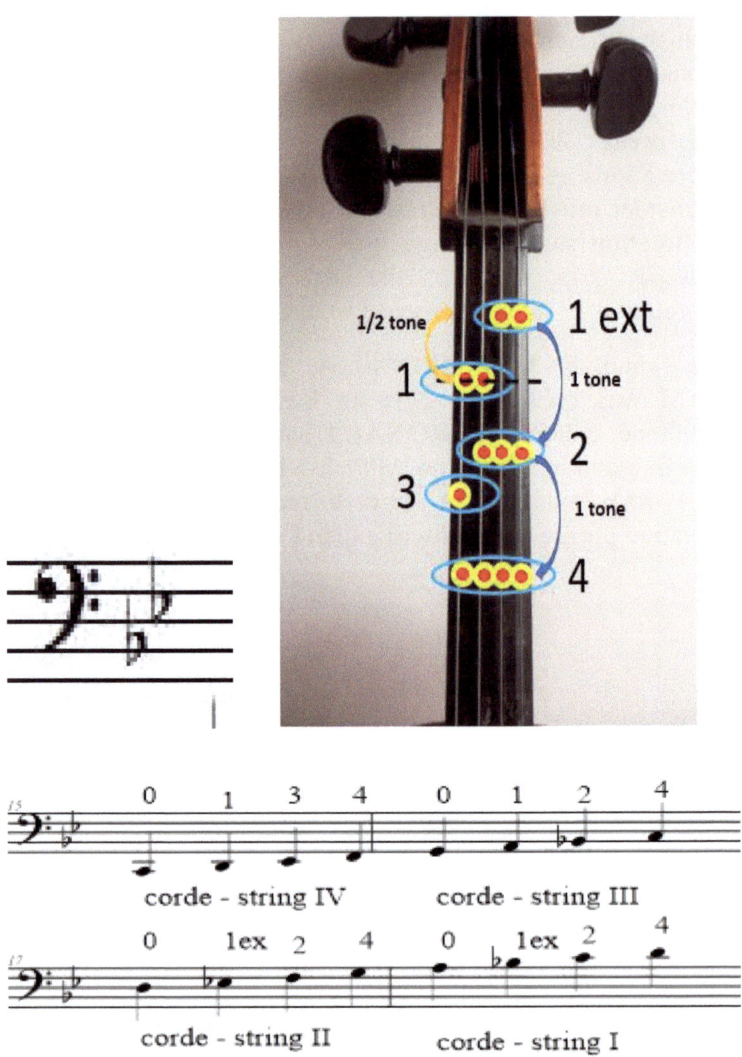

Ré major

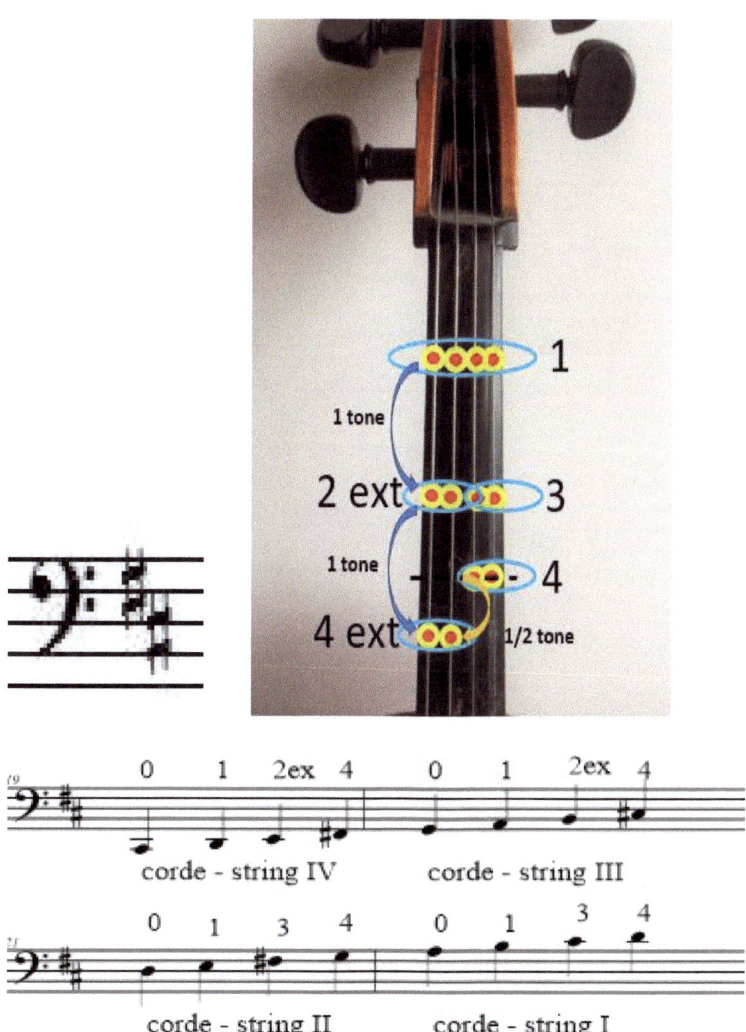

Remark : to go further on studying other scales ,you should be familiar with the 4th position.

Anatomy of the instrument

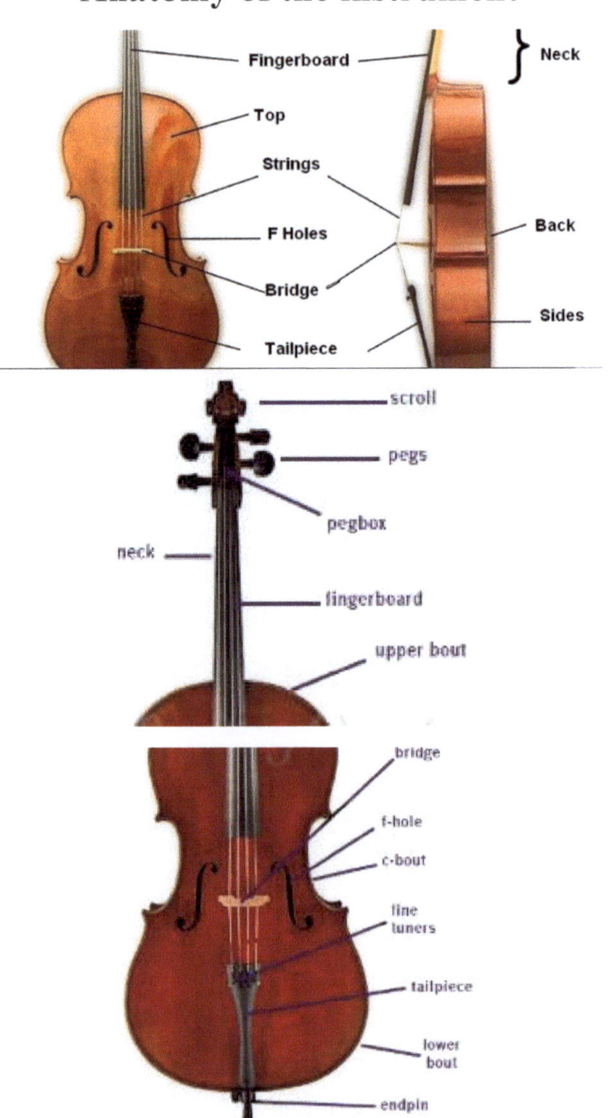

Proposals of music scores and methods

1) Method of the young cellist L.R. FEUILLARD DELRIEU edition. This is the most common method, probably the one your teacher will ask you to start. To avoid however beyond the lesson 20, because beyond, it becomes boring.

2) The ABC of the young cellist Michel TOURNUS Gérard BILLAUDOT edition. This method for children includes a CD to listen to the score you have to play. It allows to train to the correctness alone. Alternatively, any method that includes single songs with an accompanying CD may be appropriate.

3) 40 Fun studies for cello and piano or 2 cellos. Frédéric BORSARELLO Editions COMBRE. If you have the chance to be accompanied on the piano during your apprenticeship.

4) R & B classics for cello. 11 Solo Arrangements with Play Along CD. The advantage of being able to listen to the songs on a CD. If you want to play something other than classical.

5) BREVAL Leichte Stüke SCHOTT edition. A list of studies that are easy to play and nevertheless enjoyable. Use to warm up before tackling a larger piece.

6) LEE 40 Easy Studies. SCHOTT edition. Difficulty a little bigger than for the BREVAL studies.

7) Johann Christoph Friedrich Bach. Sonata in G hard and Sonata in G major for cello and basso continuo. BARENREITER edition. Two sonatas from the repertoire accessible and easy to play.

8) From BOIMORTIER Sonata in G Major for cello and string orchestra (cello and piano reduction) DELRIEU edition.

9) From BOIMORTIER Sonata in E minor for solo cello and 2 cellos SCHOTT edition.

10) J.B. BREVAL Concertino II in C major for cello and piano. Review L.R. FEUILLARD. DELRIEU edition.

11) J.B. BREVAL Concertino 5 for cello and piano. Revision L.R. FEUILLARD DELRIEU edition.

12) SCHAFFRATH Sonata in G Major for cello and basso continuo Hugo Ruf. SCHOTT edition.

13) J.S. BACH Suites for solo cello. Wiener Urtext Edition. SCHOTT Universal Edition. The 6 suites of Bach. A must, even if only the first three are accessible.

14) D. GABRIELLI. Complete works for cello. HORTUS MUSICUS. Baroque music very pleasant to play and to hear containing 7 ricercars and 2 sonatas.

15) SCHUMANN Fantasy for cello op. 73. Version for cello. Edition G. Henle Verlag. It's very difficult but so beautiful!

Some scores that can be downloaded (especially from the MUSESCORE website)

16) Anonymous GREENSLEEVES. Arrangement by Paul Fleury. Easy to start.

17) LULLY Astrée Partition of Phaeton and Astrée troupe. Nice piece of character.

18) HANDEL Cantate HWV 91 a.

19) SCHUBERT andante OP 100 of the Concerto in F Major. Well known air borrowed by Stanley Kubrick in Barry Lindon.

20) CORELLI Concerto grosso op 6. A lot of character. Difficult but it's worth it!

21) VIVALDI Concerto for cellos in major DO. For 2 cellos. Easy if you play the part of accompaniment.

22) RAMIN DJAWADI Game of Thrones including the Rain of Castamere, Winterfell. For 1 or 2 cellos.

Scores dedicated for beginners

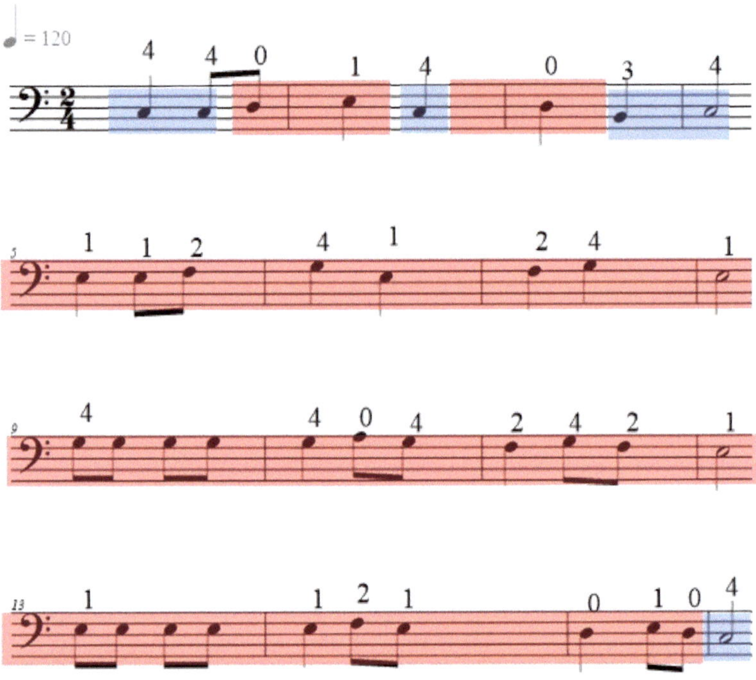

Remark: One color on the score means that the notes have to be played with the same string.

For starting, please play with the beat of 60 instead of 120.

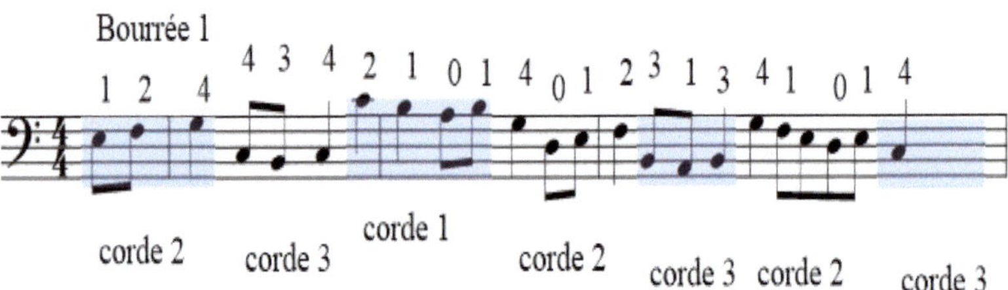

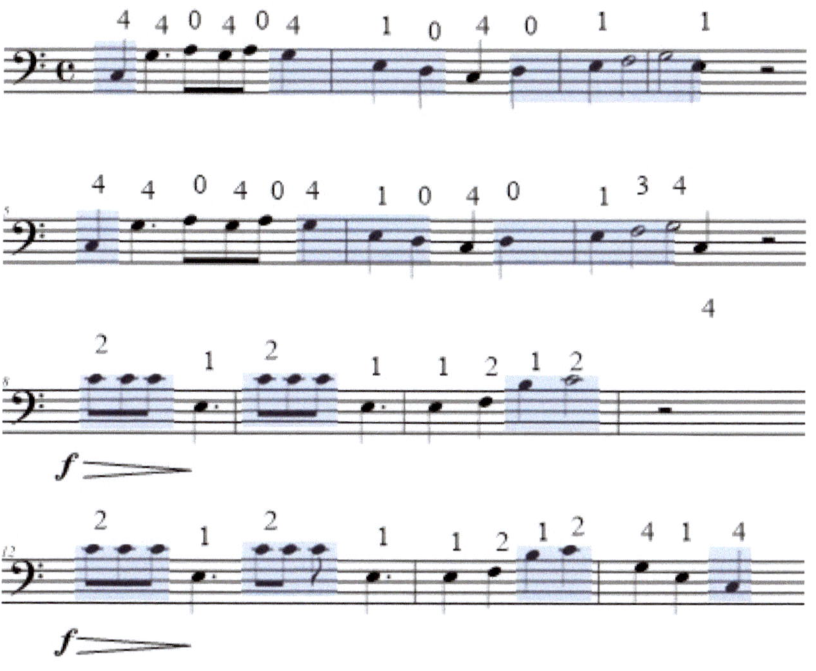

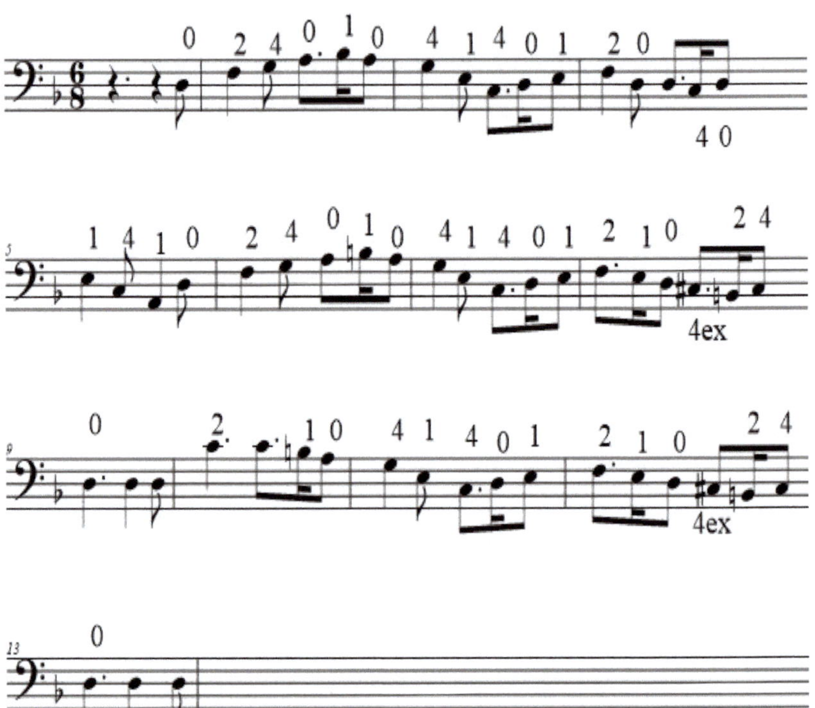

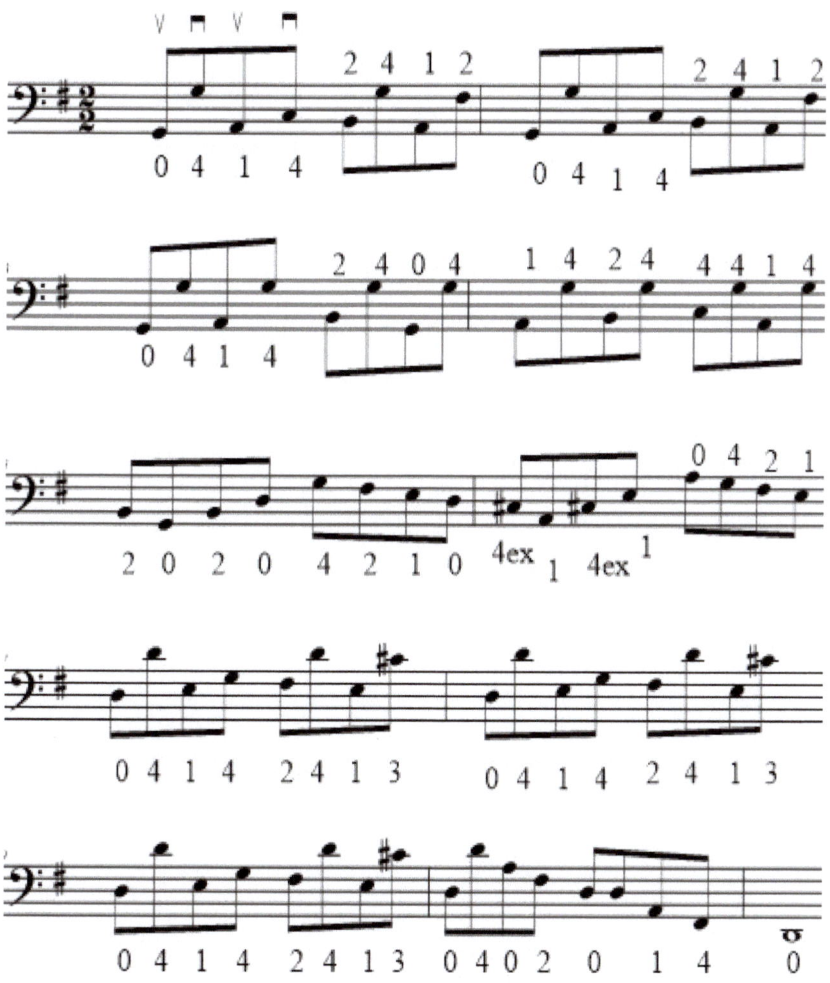

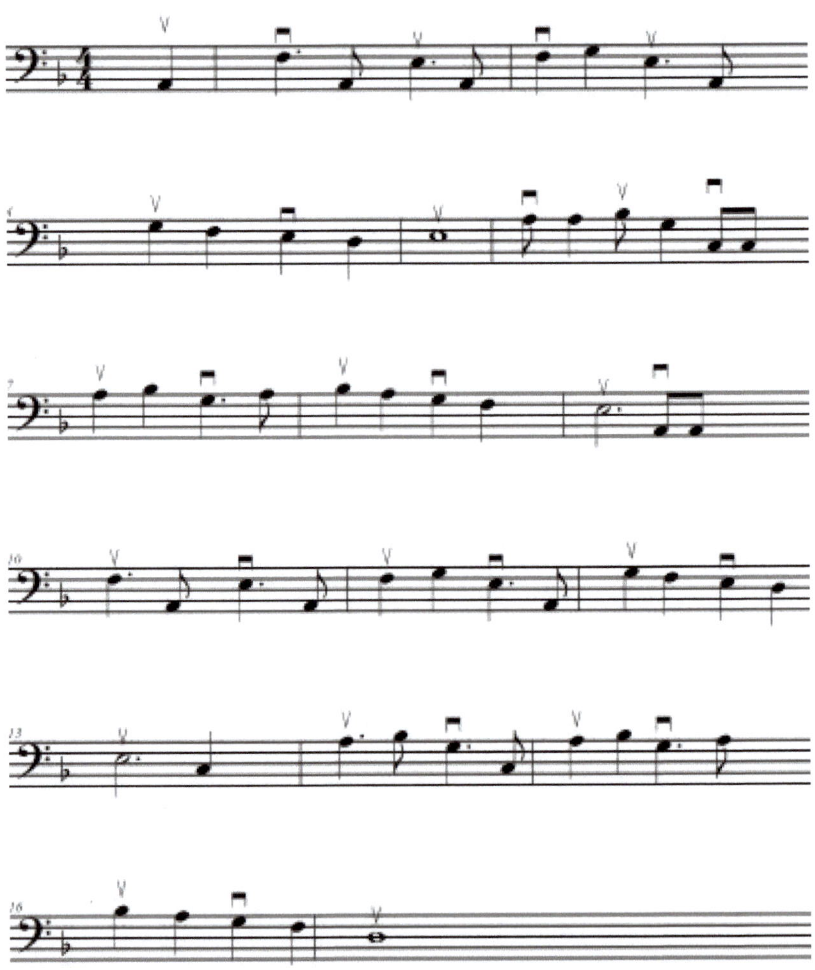

Remark: bow movement training to gain rhythm

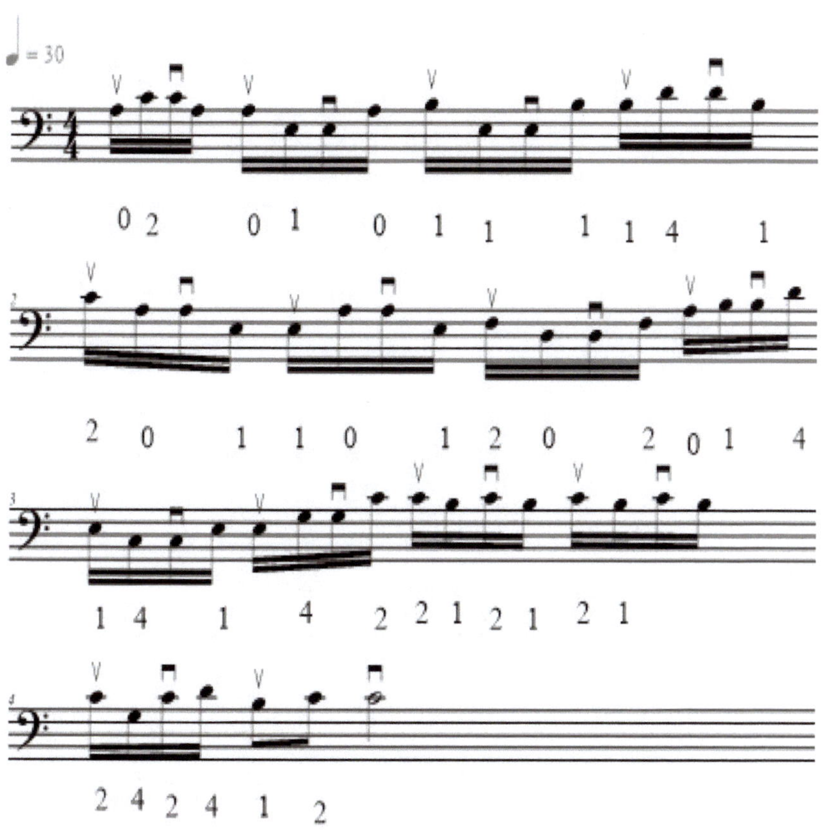

= 30
V
0 2 0 1 0 1 1 1 1 4 1
V
2 0 1 1 0 1 2 0 2 0 1 4
V
1 4 1 4 2 2 1 2 1 2 1
V
2 4 2 4 1 2

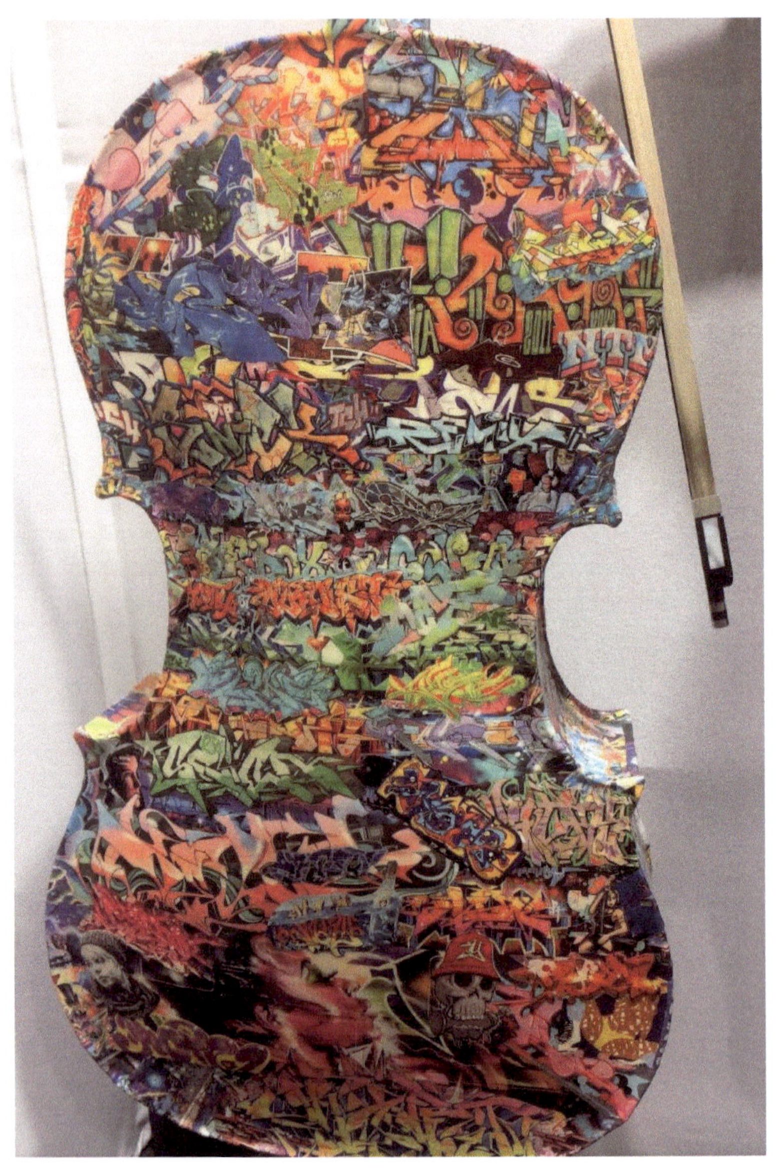